George Ratcliffe Woodward

Legends of the saints

George Ratcliffe Woodward

Legends of the saints

ISBN/EAN: 9783337150037

Printed in Europe, USA, Canada, Australia, Japan

Cover: Foto ©ninafisch / pixelio.de

More available books at **www.hansebooks.com**

LEGENDS OF THE SAINTS

BY

The Rev. G. R. WOODWARD

OF S. BARNABAS, PIMLICO

LONDON
KEGAN PAUL, TRENCH, TRÜBNER & CO. Ltd.
1898

CONTENTS

I.—LEGENDS OF THE SAINTS

	PAGE
Legend of Saint Christopher	1
Saint Joyce's Loaf of Bread	20
Saint Austin and the Angel-Child	23
Saint Ursula	24
Saint Nicolas	25
Saint Laurence, Deacon and Martyr	27
Saint Martin, Bishop of Tours	29
St. George the Martyr	32
St. George and the Dragon	34
King Eric's Faith	39
Salve Trophaeum Gloriae	42

II.—OTHER VERSES

Esay's Vision	47
Jesus and the Moss	48
Saint John and the Little Worm	50
Belshazzar's Feast	52
Die Eile der Zeit in Gott	54

	PAGE
WACHET AUF, RUFFT UNS DIE STIMME	59
GOOD CHRISTEN MEN, 'TIS TIME TO SING	61
A CHRISTMAS TREE	64
IN CRUCIS PENDENS STIPITE	66
HOLY CHURCH MUST RAISE THE LAY	68
CHRISTUS PRO NOBIS PASSUS EST	70
TO-DAY WE TELL THE STORY	71
GOD IS GONE UP ON HIGH TO-DAY	74
HARVEST-SONG	75
SPINN, MÄDCHEN, SPINN	77
SUMMER	79
A PRAYER TO BE SAID ON GOING TO BED	83

III.—THE LEGEND OF SAINT DOROTHY

THE LEGEND OF SAINT DOROTHY, VIRGIN AND MARTYR	87

I
LEGENDS OF THE SAINTS

LEGEND OF SAINT CHRISTOPHER

IN Palestine, long time ago,
There dwelt a certain Offero:
A giant he, full gaunt and grim,
A relic of the Anakim,
Whom God commanded Israel
Forth out of Canaan to expel;
Since Goliah of Gath, I ween,
Than he none stronger had been seen.
This Offero was from his youth
A man of war, to say the sooth,
That ne'er was taught to write nor read,
Nor give to books of learning heed.
But all his pleasure and delight
Was but to wrestle or to fight;
Of pagan parents born and bred,
A pagan life in youth he led.
Time came when, wearying of home,
Abroad his fancy was to roam,
And seek if haply he might find
Some king, according to his mind,
In might, in riches and in worth,
The greatest monarch upon earth.
Then up and off with giant stride
He journeyeth both far and wide,

Until at length he reached a town,
Where dwelt a king of great renown.
Spake Offero—' King live for ever!
Some time ago I did me sever
From kith and kindred, house and home,
To seek a king in heathendome
Or Christentie, o'er all the rest
The powerfullest, wisest, best.
Thee therefore I would gladly serve,
From path of duty ne'er to swerve.'
The king and eke his nobles all,
Assembled in the banquet hall,
Much marvellèd to see a man
In height four cubits and a span,
With stalwart arms and sinews strong,
With thigh and breast-bone broad and long.
' Be welcome,' quoth the king at length,
' A second Samson thou for strength.
Good Offero, thine offer free
We here accept, and thou shalt be
Our faithful squire and trusty knight,
And take the fore-front in the fight.'

Befel it so upon a day,
A certain harper came that way
And stood before our comely king,
None better ever harpt on string.
An olden song he sang by note
The words according to the rote,
Now while he sang it came to pass
When e'er the name of Sathanas

Was spoken by the harper sweet,
The king, upon his royal seat,
Devoutly and before the rest,
Each time did trace upon his breast
A certain sign, as though in awe.
This Offero the heathen saw.
So when the minstrel's song was done,
Or e'er another was begun,
The Giant he full fain would know
Wherefore and why the king did so.
Whereon the king in answer spake
'That holy sign in faith I make
To guard me, soul and body, well
From Sathanas, the fiend of hell,
Of whose assault and craft and spite
Hourly I stand in sore affright,
For know thou, could he have his will,
He would us, men and women, kill.'
Then spake Sir Offero in scorn
' I quit thy court to-morrow morn ;
Of Sathanas to stand in fear
Is argument and proof full clear
That thou art not, as people state,
On earth the greatest potentate.
No more thy servant then deceive ;
Thy service straightway I must leave,
And hence go seek this prince of pride,
And find where he and his abide ;
For by thine own admittance now
He is a mightier king than thou.'

So Offero, ere break of day,
Is gone again upon his way,
A travelling in search and quest
Of Sathanas by east or west.
He had not very far to go
Nor make a lengthy search, for lo!
Upon that day, at eventide,
He looked and straight ahead espied
A mighty host of armèd men
Came marching o'er the marshy fen,
Their royal banners gleam afar,
For they are marching on to war.
And all the troop is well be-dight
With scimitar and dagger bright,
A quiver full of arrows keen,
On every soldier might be seen.
Well armed were they from top to toe,
Their number nobody doth know;
In uniform of scarlet hue,
The host was clad, and sombre blue—
In stature all were tall, and strong:
No weakling, none in all that throng;
And to the sound of musick gay,
Ionian, the sooth to say,
With pipe and tabour, flute and drum,
In serried ranks they onward come.
Before this host a Captain went,
He, like his men on conquest bent,
With air and circumstance and state
Of one that was a victor great.
But he was taller than the rest,

And in more gaudy raiment drest,
And on his marches far and wide,
While others walkt, himself would ride.
Upon a steed as black as jet
This mighty General was set.
Right glad was Offero to see
As grand an army as might be,
But as they near and nearer drew
Dread thoughts of doubt within him grew:
About their look, to tell the truth,
Was something weird, unkind, uncouth.
Thought Offero, birds of one feather,
As saith the proverb, flock together.
Now seeing such an ugly crew,
He would have fled in moments few
Had not the Commandant-in-chief,
Observing quick his pain and grief,
Leapt from the saddle to the ground.
'Whence camest thou and whither bound,
My man?' quoth he to Offero,
'Thy name and country I would know.'
While thus he spake, with fair intent,
It seemèd like a compliment
To Offero that one so great
Should stoop to men of low estate;
And after all, on closer sight,
The Chief was like some Angel bright.
'My lord, my name is Offero,
Afar I wander to and fro
From Canäan, my native land,
To seek, if thou dost understand,

The Prince of all the world so wide
And stand for ever by his side,
Dan Sathanas he hath to name.'
' If him thou seek'st, I am the same.
No further need to search afield :
The sceptre of this world I wield.
Now join mine army, rank and file,
And I will make it worth thy while;
For thou shalt work for meat and fee,
And purchase so a good degree.
Sooth, thou art no bad specimen,
God wot, of Canaanitish men,
My old allies are they of yore,
Would I had, like them, many more !
Come therefore serve me, body, soul,
And in my ranks I thee enrol.'

He spake. Then Offero full fain,
Upon the dry and barren plain,
Fell on his knees a-grovelling
In worship of this mighty king.
And straightway gave his glad consent
To follow wheresoe'er he went.
This troop had gone a long, long way,
When so it fell upon a day
They crossed a cool and pleasant rill,
And then gan climb a steep green hill,
That stood outside a city wall ;
The city lay in ruins all.
Where road cut road at angles right,
This army saw a wonder sight.

Upon that hill-top lo! there stood
A giant Cross of cedar wood :
In view of which both Sathanas
And every one that with him was,
Save Offero, gan tremble sore
From head to foot, as men forlore.
So right about they face anon,
And quick as lightning get them gone :
They would pursue their journey still,
And yet avoid the ghastly hill,
So by a circuit through a lane
The King's own high-way they regain.

Now when the panic-stricken band
Recovered had its self-command,
And after flying many a mile,
Now thought it safe to rest awhile,
Long time in wonderment thereat
Poor Offero astonied sat,
'What aileth thee, O master mine,
That thou so fleddest, thou and thine?'
But ne'er a word his master spake
For he and his were all a-quake
So mindful of the proverb old,
'Oft speech is silver, silence gold,'
His answer to his man was 'mum' :
(In sooth,) the devil he was dumb.
Quoth Offero in haste, 'God wot,
I leave thee, an thou tell me not.'
And therefore under sore constraint
The fiend replied in accents faint;

And give the devil but his due,
That liar for the nonce spake true.
' Upon the Cross that thou didst see
On yonder mount of Calvary,
Jesus the Son of Mary died,
By Jew and Roman crucified :
I urged them to the deed alone,
I was mistaken, truth to own,
For I discover, to my cost,
Thereby souls many I have lost.
No sin, but only on my part
An error, for the which I smart,
For sure so often as I see
The sight of yon accursed tree,
I shake for fear and seem undone
Because of Jesus, Mary's son.
For him I hate, in very deed
The Son of God, the woman's seed.'

Thus Offero in quick reply
Quoth, 'Fie upon thee, Sirrah, fie,
Thou sawest but a gallow-tree,
Yet like a reed upon the lea
Thou shakest still for very fright,
And cowardly didst take to flight.
But grant thou art an armèd man,
And stronger than Leviathan,
If true thy tale, thou hast ere now
Found yet a stronger man than thou.
And that is Jesus, Mary's son,
To death by Jews and Romans done,

Whom still thou fearest, so 'tis plain,
As if he were alive again.
So Jesus now I fain would seek,
I reckon thee not worth a leek.'
Thereat the fiend and eke his flock
Of Offero made mirth and mock,
And then and there was much ado:
He would begone, but they said no,
But glad was Offero to find
When once he had made up his mind,
His steps they would no longer stay,
For where the will is, there the way.
'Besides,' thought he, 'what harm to try
And see if I may not defy
Both Sathanas and all his band.
With thumb and finger of my hand
In faith I trace the mystic sign
Made by that Christen king benign,
My former master, on the day
The harper 'fore him came to play.'
They knew the sign and straightway flee;
Thus Offero is left full free
Again to journey far and wide
In search of Christ the Crucified.
And travellers asked he every one,
To point the way to Mary's Son.
Now after many months and hours
Of honest search, through summer showers,
And winter storms, in sunshine bright,
In heat by day, and cold by night,
The giant came unto a cell

Wherein there did a hermit dwell.
A holy man and just was he,
As hermits are or ought to be;
'Good father,' thus spake Offero,
'I pray thee, of thy goodness, show
Thy servant which may be the way
To Jesus Christ, and that to-day.'
The hermit bade him welcome be,
And spake in words of courtesy
'My Son, the King whom thou dost seek,
Is mighty, merciful and meek.
No peer in all the world hath he,
The God of heaven and earth and sea,
The Lord of lords, of kings the King,
The praise of every living thing,
To wrath and anger he is slow,
But will not let the sinner go.
The mills of God grind nothing fast,
But grind exceeding small at last.
Thou wouldest serve him? well and good
But be it plainly understood,
That Jesus Christ doth often ask
His folk to do some irksome task,
Which flesh and blood by nature shun,
And would right gladly leave undone.
Yet Christens find (I rede thee right)
An easy yoke and burthen light
Is on his true disciples laid
By Jesus, Son of Mary maid.
We fast and pray.'—Quoth Offero
'Were I to fast, my strength would go.

Impossible to fast, for then
I should become as other men.
And as for falling on my knees
This practice never could me please.'
' Woe worth the day ! ' replied that other,
' Thou speakest foolishly, lief brother.
Yet favour I will ask of thee,
So, prithee, say not nay to me.
There is a river near my cell,
It cometh down from moor and fell ;
'Tis shallow in the summer-tide,
But in the winter deep and wide,
Then, what with rain and melting snow,
A mighty torrent it doth grow.
The stream is then well full of danger,
Alike to town folk and to stranger,
And many a daughter, husband, wife,
Ere now therein have lost their life.
No bridge is there, nor ferry-boat
The wayfarer across to float.
Now since thou seest not thy way
Neither to fast nor yet to pray,
My counsel is no longer roam,
But by yon river make thy home.
There turn thy strength to good account,
And aid the traveller to surmount
The perils of the swollen flood.
And hearken yet, my brother good,
For little or perchance no pay,
There be thou, ready, night and day
With staff in hand, at beck and call,

Of wayfarers, or great or small,
Who need to cross from either shore:
These take and carry safely o'er,
Upon thy back so broad and long,
Or set upon thy shoulders strong;
Then land thy burthen, safe and sound,
Upon the dry and solid ground.
If thou perform this office well
Then peradventure, who can tell,
Jesus may come to thee some day
And show thee yet a better way
Whereby to worship him aright
And walk more humbly in his sight.'

He spake and straightway Offero
Full fain made answer, 'Be it so;
I can and will obey thy rede.'
'Go,' quoth the hermit, 'God thee speed.'
Thus Offero that very day
Toward the river took his way
And chose a spot beside the ford,
According to the hermit's word,
Whereon he built, as best he might,
A cabin rude yet water-tight
And weather-proof, and there he dwelt
Alone, yet never lonely felt.
For whether it were day or night
Whene'er he spied in sorry plight
A pilgrim either young or old
Who fain would cross the waters cold,
A-shivering on the river's brink,

Or cried from mid-stream, 'Help, I sink.'
Then Offero, that giant kind,
Came to the rescue, swift as wind,
With staff in hand, both strong and good,
(It was a palm-tree of the wood,)
He sallied forth without demur
To aid the traveller, him or her,
In jeopardy: and so did save
Full many from a watery grave.
Upon this work of mercy bent,
When many days he now had spent,
It came to pass upon a night
While he was taking slumber light
Upon the bed-straw in his room
(His lamp gone out, and thick the gloom)
He suddenly awoke and hark!
Outside his cabin, in the dark,
He heard the voice, as of a child,
That called him o'er the waters wild,
'For pity's sake, for charity,
Come, o'er the stream, come carry me.'
Then Offero, as quick as thought,
Arose from sleep and straightway sought
His lanthorn, for there was no moon,
Girt up his loins, did on his shoon,
Unsparred the door, and staff in hand
Went out toward the river-strand.
The night was dark and o'er the hill
Euroclydon blew cold and chill,
But though he searchèd well around,
No child could anywhere be found;

So homeward he, through darkness deep,
And laid him down again to sleep.
But though he fain would slumber take,
His heart, nathless, still kept awake.
And hark in little time again,
Above the whistling wind and rain,
Above the water-flood hard by,
Was heard the very self-same cry
' Help Offero, for charity,
Come o'er the stream, come carry me.'
Again he rose to sally forth,
Looked east and west, looked south and north,
And though he called aloud, around,
' Say, where thou mayest, child, be found.'
Yet fruitless was his search and vain,
So to his cabin he again.
Him thought, ' Perchance 'tis but a dream,
That voice that called me to the stream,
Or, if it be a voice at all,
'Tis done in mockery withal
By somebody on joking set,
Some man who would my slumber let,
On such a wintry night and cold,
When winds blow chill o'er wood and wold,
No child, of woman born and bred,
Can be abroad, and not abed,
Wherefore, I straightway go to rest,
Nought shall my slumber more molest.'
He laid him down, but hark! again
A child gan call, in accents plain,
' Help Offero, for charity,

Come o'er the stream and carry me.'
Sweet was the voice, but sad of tone,
Unutterably woe-begone.
In sooth, it was a little child,
Abroad that night in weather wild,
Whose plaintive voice, as with a dart
Did pierce the Giant to the heart.
Anon he rose from where he lay,
The third time now ere dawn of day.
He listened well and looked around
And heard—'twas no uncertain sound—
A child upon the other shore
Was calling, 'Come, come quickly o'er.'
So with his staff, like weaver's beam,
Good Offero gan ford the stream,
And landing on the further side
A wonder sight he there espied,
Above the bank upon a stone,
In need of help there sat alone
A gentle Child, so fair of face,
And altogether full of grace.
'Ah! woe is me, poor Child, for thee.'
Quoth Offero, for kind was he
By nature, and of tender heart,
'Child, prithee tell me who thou art,
Thy name and errand I would know,
Thy father's name and home also.'
Then spake the Child, the self-same tide;
'The river runneth deep and wide,
First bear me o'er the swollen flood
And I will give thee answer good.

Then Offero full tenderly
Knelt down upon his bended knee,
And lift aloft the youngling small
Upon his shoulders strong and tall.
Thus down the bank and grassy sedge,
They quickly reach the river's edge,
And now good Offero full fain
Doth through the water wade again:
But when that they in mid-stream were,
The giant and the babe so fair,
Scarce Offero could keep his feet,
The torrent seemed to run so fleet,
And deeper now the eddies grew,
And stronger still the whirl-wind blew,
The Babe too on his shoulders set
Waxed heavy and more heavy yet,
So that the staff within his hand
Such strain no longer well might stand,
It was belike to break asunder.
Thus Offero began to wonder,
By reason of his failing strength,
If he should gain the bank at length,
Or else be drownèd in the wave,
With nobody at hand to save.
His shoulders 'neath their load did bow,
But on he went, he wot not how,
Until at last, by might and main,
He struggled to dry land again,
And then, his perils safely o'er,
He stood a while upon the shore,
He panted fast, his strength was spent,

For once he knew what languor meant.
Adown he sat upon the grass,
And took the infant, as he was,
With either arm his neck around,
And set him too upon the ground.
No mother greater care could show
To babe than worthy Offero.
When he had gotten breath to speak,
He cried, 'Thou stranger child, so meek,
Who didst me in much peril place,
Now prithee tell me, of thy grace,
Who art thou? and from whence art come?
And whither journeyest thou home?
What brought thee out so late to-night,
Thus lonely and in sorry plight,
When bloweth wind from north and east,
Night fit for neither man nor beast?
Of all the folk I ever bare
Across the stream, none may compare
With thee for weight, thou tiny child,
Above all other meek and mild.
A mountain on my back methought
With thee, I verily had brought.'
Then answer made the Child full free,
' No marvel, Offero,' quoth he,
' That thou so heavy didst me find :
I made the world and all mankind—
The pillars of the earth so fair,
Th' inhabiters thereof I bear.
Christ-child am I ; as thou hast borne
The Saviour Christ, this stormy morn,

The God of heaven and earth and sea,
Not Offero thy name shall be.
The world henceforward shall thee know
By thy new name Christofero.
From heaven above, where I do dwell,
I saw thy love and noted well
Thy many deeds of charity,
The which well pleasing were to me.
And though thou knewest not aright
How to be perfect in my sight,
Thy service I did not disdain.
Now if thou wilt my praise obtain,
Go seek yon hermit in the wood,
And do as him it seemeth good.
And suffer him to Christen thee
In name of holy Trinity,
Repenting of thy sins of old,
Exceeding great and manifold,
Then go into the world to teach,
My word to heathen people preach,
For many souls from darksome night
Thou mayest lead to realms of light.
And if thou doubtest here my word,
Christofero, I am the Lord.
Lo! hereby give I thee a token
That I the very sooth have spoken.
The staff thou holdest in thy hand,
Go take and plant it on the land:
And though it be so dry a stick,
Yet it shall bud and blossom thick
With leaves and dates in proper season.

Thy hearers fain will know the reason,
Then say how, once upon a night,
Thou foundest, and in wretched plight,
A Child, whom thou didst bear across
A river wide (not to thy loss),
With that same staff thou barest o'er
Thy Lord and God from shore to shore.'

SAINT JOYCE'S LOAF OF BREAD

(*L. Th. Kosegarten.*)

To prove his servant's love (so legends say)
Our Saviour Jesus Christ did come one day
Disguisèd in a common beggar's smock,
And at Saint Joyce's door did stand and knock,
And humbly crave a crust of household bread:
Saith Joyce, 'Go, steward, see this comeling fed.'
'But one loaf, Sir, in pantry can be found,
'Then what is left for master, man and hound?'
'Give ne'er the less,' the worthy Abbot cried,
'Give, alway give, God surely will provide.'
With knife the steward doth exactly mete
And quarter the remaining loaf of wheat.
One fourthing gave he to the beggar man,
To whom in friendly wise he thus began:
'See, this is thine: and this Lord Abbot's share,
'And this my own, and this the mastiff's fare.'
Saint Joyce gan smile, and off the beggar went.
Soon after, clad in worse habiliment,
Our Lord before the Abbey-gate again
Doth ask for bread. Quoth good Saint Joyce full fain,
'Another stranger? Let him have my bit:

'God will provide, and so saith Holy Writ.'
'Twas done; but soon in outward form and frame
Of one that was an-hungered sore he came,
The Lord, the third time now in want of bread,
'My piece is gone, but give him thine instead,'
Saith Joyce unto his steward at that tide,
'Nought shall we lack, the Lord he will provide.'
Yet once again the Saviour Jesus came,
Now blind and naked, destitute and lame.
The fourth time he did crave for food to eat,
'Go steward, let him have the mastiff's meat.
'He who doth feed the ravens when they cry
'Assuredly our wants will satisfy.'
The loaf, their all is spent; the beggar gone;
When hark! a heavenly voice is heard anon,
'Great is thy faith, disciple true: so be
'It done, as thou believest, unto thee.'
Eftsoon a wondrous sight the steward spied
From out the lattice: by the river side
Not very far away, lo! galleys four
Came sailing, nay discharging on the shore
Their precious cargo, fruit, oil, wine and bread;
With joy the eager steward thither sped:
No crew saw he: but on the bank, behold,
A pennon white with letters writ in gold,
'Unto the Abbot who to-day hath given
'Bread, four times over, to the king of heaven,
'The Lord who giveth hungry ravens food,

'Doth send these galleys four with cargo good:
'One for the Abbot, good Saint Joyce by name,
'And one his faithful Steward here may claim,
'And one the mastiff: as for number four,
''Tis for the Donor's brethren, sick and poor.'

SAINT AUSTIN AND THE ANGEL-CHILD

As good Saint Austin on a day
Along the sea-shore took his way,
He spied a boy upon the strand,
Digging and delving in the sand,
As silly child for ever will.
The Bishop looked and then stood still.
' Why dig that hole?' Saint Austin said,
' What mean thy bucket, shell and spade?'
' Herein I hope in time,' quoth he,
' To pour the waters of the sea.'
' No easy work, thou gentle child;
' Impossible,' the Bishop smiled.
' Yet, learnèd teacher, Augustine,
' Far simpler is my task than thine;
' A book thou writest, so think me,
' About the Blessed Trinitye.
' But I can drain yon ocëan
' More easily than thou, O Man,
' Canst skill to fathom here aright
' The mysteries of God Almight.'
Now ere the Saint could think thereon,
Behold! the angel-child was gone.

SAINT URSULA

Wackernagel v. 1541.

℣. Saint Ursula doth cross the sea,
   Of noble English race was she;

℣. Within her barque, so deeply laden,
   There sail eleven thousand maiden.

℣. O virgin-band, with souls (God wot)
   Pure as the sun, without a spot.

℣. O ship, with freight and cargo good,
   Crown, palm-branch, wreathlet, dart and blood.

℣. No merchant-vessel ever bare
   From Ind such goodly pearls and rare.

℣. Ope soon thy portal, welkin kind,
   And speed the ship with favouring wind.

℟. Maid Ursula, now as of yore,
   Be likewise thou our commodore,
   And land us on the heavenly shore.

SAINT NICOLAS

Des Knaben Wunderhorn p. 791.

Father. Of good Saint Nicolas of old
      Our forefathers this legend told,
      That he doth come from Moscow town,
      Where he is held in great renown :
      Already he is on his way,
      A visit to our schools to pay,
      See how our children, every one,
      Have through the year their lessons done,
      And how they read, write, sing and pray,
      And know if they be good or nay.
      He carrieth upon his back
      Of sugar-candy dolls a sack,
      And other such-like pretty toys,
      His prizes for good girls and boys.

Child. I pray thee, good Saint Nicolas,
      On no account our school-room pass.
      But come with book or coat or shoe,
      And other lovely things thereto.
      So I will learn my task for thee,
      And be as good as good can be.   Amen.

Saint Nicolas. God bless you, children, lief and
              dear,
  Obey your parents, and revere.
  Thus shall ye win a present here.
  But play the fool and anger God,
  And I do bring you stick and rod.
  Amen.

SAINT LAURENCE, DEACON AND MARTYR

Apostolorum supparem—Daniel's Thesaurus,
Vol. i. f. 103.

LAURENCE th' Archdeacon's feast is here,
Of Paul or Peter all but peer:
For he at Rome, that famous town,
Won, as did they, a martyr's crown.

As blessed Xystus neared the stake,
Sure word of prophecy he spake:
'Refrain thy tears, my Son,' quod he,
'In three days thou shalt follow me.'

Fearless of pain Saint Laurence stood,
To learn his legacy of blood:
And calmly faced, without dismay,
The debt, that soon himself should pay.

E'en now, to see his Bishop slain,
Made Laurence feel a martyr's pain:
His title deeds in blood-red ink,
The father's cup the heir shall drink.

In three days came the stern behest,
'Fetch treasures out of Church and Chest.'
'It shall be done, said he, to-day.'
Thus to his triumph adding play.

O lovely sight and noble thought!
A crowd of beggars Laurence brought:
'Look round, sir Prefect, an ye please,
The treasures of the Church be these.'

'The poor and needy, near and far,
Of Holy Church the riches are.'
Thus mocked, the greedy foe in ire
Bade gridiron fetch and kindle fire.

But see the fireman leave his post,
And, scorched himself, give up the ghost.
'Well done, turn roast the other side,
The feast is cooked,' St Laurence cried.

St Ambrose or Ambrosian.

SAINT MARTIN, BISHOP OF TOURS

'Touching Martin,' Satan said,
'Fiends of hell, be not afraid,
Dread nought, only hark and hear,
To your Master's rede give ear:
Martin, who attacked and taunted,
Still continueth undaunted,
Obstinate, who, to our scorn,
Leadeth back again all manner
Men and women from our banner
To the hateful Virgin-born:
Worth our while his power to shatter.
So in hand I take the matter,
He is one of us by morn.'

As the lying spirit spake,
Form and body he gan take,
Did the Saviour counterfeit,
Countenance and dress complete.
'Fear not ye, my trusty crew,
Though yon hateful form ye view
Fear not ye, in any wise;
Tush, I am the same as ever,
Old my hatred dieth never

Though I don his form and guise.
To 'Saint' Martin, ne'er so wary,
I shall seem the Son of Mary,
Martin's soul shall be my prize.

Prinked in purple robe of state,
Like some earthly potentate,
Crown on head Apollyon,
Proud and insolent, set on.
Terror-struck these guilty creatures,
Viewing e'en those feignèd features,
Weylaway! aloud gan cry:
Howling fled that crowd infernal,
Seeking rest in fires eternal,
'Fore the Lord's avenging arm.
Even Satan, arch-blasphemer,
In the garb of man's Redeemer
Shook full sore in dread alarm.

Meantime Bishop Martin see
Full of faith, hope, charity
Self-forgetting, humble, leal,
At his crucifix doth kneel.
'Thou who diedest for mankind,
Save and see us from the Fiend.
Bound by cords of sin we be,
Strive not with us in thy wrath,
Cleanse us in thy mercy's bath.
Come from sin to set us free.'

And there came the Prince of lies,
Satan in the form and guise

SAINT MARTIN

Of the world's Redeemer he.
Clad in purple robe of state,
Like some earthly potentate,
Proud and insolent, anon
Spake that Prince Apollyon.
'Martin, I am Christ and lo!
Verily myself I show,
Where men fall and worship me:
Wherefore I command thee now
Openly before me bow,
Manifest in flesh to thee.'
Martin started, oped his eyes,
Half in anger, half surprise,
Viewed his guest, but nought said he.

Him again the Fiend addrest,
'Christ am I, hear my behest.
Only kneel a-down before me.
And with heart and soul adore me.'
'Christ in mercy,' spake that other,
'Came on earth, the poor man's brother,
Christ the very Truth and Light:
He upon the gibbet died
Thou art come in robes of pride.
Fiend, ✠ I know thee not, away!'
Thus 'twas known to be a lie.
Martin, blessing God on high,
Sinless on the pavement lay.

ADELBERT VON CHAMISSO.

ST. GEORGE THE MARTYR

Gesta sanctorum Martyrum—Mone, III. f. 315.

It is a good and joyful thing
The deeds of martyr-saints to sing:
For when the servant's fame we tell
The master's name is praised as well.

George, warrior of Jesus sworn,
In Cappadocia bred and born,
Did earthly vanities despise,
And made of heaven merchandize.

In value pounds and pence, I ween,
George reckoned barely worth a bean:
But rich in faith and love of God
The poor he fed and clothed and shod.

Came order from the kingly throne
To worship idols, wood and stone:
Which he, like Christen knight, and true,
Into the depths of deep sea threw.

The King, in fierce and angry wise,
Sore punishment then gan devise.
Scourge, chains and shackles, rack and wheel,
Gridiron, bars and bolts of steel.

But nought this Confessor dismayed,
For Jesus lent his servant aid :
George for the people more and more
The fruits of grace supernal bore.

Queen Alexandria, by name,
Soon won, through him, a martyr's fame :
Low under foot the world she trod,
And merited a crown of God.

For seven long years in pain and woe
George laid the Prince of earth full low :
Then, 'headed by the foeman's sword,
Enter'd the joy of Christ his Lord.

ST GEORGE AND THE DRAGON

Des Knaben Wunderhorn, p. 103.

W<small>ITHIN</small> a cavern on a fen
A fierce old dragon had his den,
The dread of all, north, south, and east,
Alike devouring man and beast:
The breath of whose twin nostrils wide
Did taint the air on every side.
For safety, both of hearth and hall,
The Senators decreed withal
To turn adrift two sheep a day
To keep the dreadful pest away.
When no more sheep were left in pen,
Another plan they thought on then;
A human being, free or thrall,
Must go, on whom the lot should fall.
In course of time, the truth to tell,
The lot upon the Princess fell.
The King his people summonèd:
'I give you half my realm instead,
In gold or silver, coin or kind,
Choose that for which ye have a mind.
My only daughter! God forefend,
My heiress come to such an end!'

The folk 'gan cry aloud in fere:
' But other hold their children dear:
Thou canst not, for thy daughter's sake,
Break laws that thou thyself didst make:
Do, and we burn, within a stound,
Thee and thy palace to the ground.'
No idle threat the King perceived,
He spake in anger, inly grieved;
' Allow me time, eight days of grace
To mourn my daughter's hapless case.'
Then spake he to his daughter mild,
' Ah, daughter dear, my darling Child,
So I must stand and see thee die,
And end my days in misery.'
Now when th' appointed time was past,
The mob ran to the palace fast
With instant threat of sword and fire,
And shouts, as if to glut their ire:
' Wilt thou, to let thy daughter live,
Thy people to the dragon give?'
When otherwise it might not be,
Forced was the Monarch to agree.
He clothed his child in robes of state,
And gazed and gazed disconsolate.
' Ah! wo is me, unhappy wight,
To stand in miserable plight.
'Twas in my mind, with pomp and state
Thy wedding soon to celebrate,
With cymbal, shawm, and gay sautrie
To add unto our game and glee.
But now, thou must be sent away,

To be this gruesome dragon's prey.
Would God I were already dead,
Sooner than see thy life-blood shed!'
He kissed his darling, chin and cheek.
Before him knelt his daughter meek.
'Lief father mine, good-bye, good-bye,
'Tis sweet *pro patria mori.*'
The parting o'er, this Princess fair
Is led toward the dragon's lair;
She sat her down to sob and cry,
When George the Knight came riding by
'Hail! gentle maid, I fain would know
The reason of thy grief and woe.'
Quoth she, 'Sir, quickly get thee gone,
Lest two folk die, instead of one.'
'Nay, maiden fair; nay, fear not thou,
But briefly tell me further now
Why art thou left alone to cry,
When many people live close by?'
'Withouten doubt,' quod she, 'thou art
A perfect gentle knight at heart.
Yet wherefore wouldst thou stay to die,
And share my death of agony?'
Then soon she made him understand
How matters stood within that land.
Whereon he spake, that noble Knight,
'Take courage, maid, allay thy fright,
By aid of Jesus, God's dear Son,
A deed of prowess shall be done.'
She warned him oft, yet firm stood he.
The noisome beast came presentlye.

ST GEORGE AND THE DRAGON

'Fly, fly, sir Knight, escape full fain,
Why die, in manhood's prime, in vain?'
The Knight is up and on his steed,
And monster-ward gan spur in speed.
Like Christen Knight, the Cross so blest
He traced devoutly on his breast,
Then charging quick with trusty spear
He gave the beast a wound severe.
The Knight then knelt upon his knee,
To say, '*Non nobis, Domine!*'
Then spake he to the maiden fair,
'The beast no more shall see his lair.
Let nothing, maiden, thee dismay;
Around his neck thy girdle lay.'
She did so, and the Knight soon found
He followed like domestic hound.
He led him t'ward the city gate,
Men fled before them, small and great.
Thereon the Knight 'gan wave his arm:
'Sirs, tarry there, and dread no harm.
Lo! hither was I sent, that so
The truth of God ye now may know.
Now, if ye will baptizèd be
Becoming Christen, he and she,
I will the deadly dragon kill,
And help you drive away this ill.'
These heathen all, by God's free grace,
The Christen faith did soon embrace.
Then good Saint George his sabre drew,
And on the earth the dragon slew.
This man of God the king did offer

Much gold and silver out of coffer,
But this our hero would not have,
But to the sick and needy gave.
Now ere Saint George went on his way
Thus to the Monarch he did say,
'The Church of Christ, neglect her never;
Be she your care and charge for ever.'
With zeal the grateful Prince did raise,
To God and to our Lady's praise,
A large and lovely Church, and lo!
Therefrom a springing-well 'gan flow.

KING ERIC'S FAITH

(In Stadt Upsala's Kirche.)—*J. Gabriel Seidl.*
(Haus Schatz, p. 407.)

In fair Upsala's minster
  The Altar high is dight
With candlesticks refulgent
  And tapers clear and bright.
Before the nether foot-pace,
  Uplifting holy hands,
The king of Sweden, Eric
  In festal raiment stands.

'Lord, they who seek thy succour
  In peace and safety dwell:
With Jesus for our fellow,
  Then all with us is well.'
Thus he and all his people
  In nave and chancel wide,
'What man on earth can harm us,
  If God be on our side?'

Thus they their bedes were bidding,
  When through the Quire there sped
A messenger all breathless,
  In dust be-smotherèd.

'Good God! The Dane Skalater
  Doth march upon our town,
Seven hundred strong, his armies
  Swoop from the hills adown.'

Then cried that godly monarch,
  On hearing what befell,
' Lord, they who seek thy succour
  In peace and safety dwell.'
Then came another foot-man,
  And panting like the first,
'Skalater on the rampart,
  The last door-bar is burst.'

Undaunted still sang Eric,
  When he this news heard tell,
' Lord, they who seek thy succour,
  In peace and safety dwell.'
Yet came a third with tidings,
  But ere he spake a word,
His head fell from his body
  Struck by some Danish sword.

Ah! what a din and uproar,
  And wild alarm to boot!
Like mad-man will Skalater
  The faith of Christ up-root,
Skalater the fanatic,
  And seven hundred men.
All up with Church and sovran
  And Swede in town or fen.

That instant took king Eric
  The golden cross full bright,
And lift the same t'ward heaven,
  And waved it left and right.
From each of seven wound-prints
  Of Jesus Christ apace
There shone a hundred sun-beams
  Full in the foemen's face.

Down fell the seven hundred,
  And on their faces prone
Call from the deep in silence,
  And Christ for Master own.
While Eric and his people
  The praise of Jesus tell:
'All they who seek his succour
  In peace and safety dwell.'

SALVE TROPHAEUM GLORIAE

St Andrew's address to his Cross—Ven. Bede,
Eighth cent.

Hail! blissful trophy, noble tree!
Hail! sacred sign of victory!
Whereon the Lord to die was fain,
And ransom lost mankind again.

O Cross, O tree of glory bright,
With virtues manifold bedight:
Upon thine arms a certain day
The Body fair of Jesus lay.

Time was when every mother's son
The ghastly look of thee would shun:
But now thou art the boast and pride
Of Christendom, both far and wide.

To faithful folk a joy it is,
The holy sign to trace and kiss:
Thou, Cross, art parent of all bliss,
The key to open Paradise.

For His sweet sake, thy Cross-beams are
Than Hybla's honey sweeter far:
No honours of the world so fair
Can with the Cross of Christ compare.

Thrice happy now myself I count
Upon thy transverse arms to mount:
Thee too mine arms would fain embrace,
The ladder to a brighter place.

Then gently lift me up withal,
Kind Cross, for I am Jesu's thrall:
My Master, Christ, by aid of thee,
O tree of glory, died for me.

Thus Andrew spake the self-same tide
That he his Cross erect espied:
Guard, men of death, his robes a time,
The tree of life till Andrew climb.

II
OTHER VERSES

ESAY'S VISION

Isaiah vi. 1-4.

THE year that King Ozia died,
Esay, the prophet at that tide,
In wonderment and mickle awe,
A memorable vision saw.
Upon a high and lofty throne
There sat the LORD, the Holy One:
His robes with train and border wide
The temple filled on every side.
Above it stood a Seraph pair,
And each of them six wings did bear:
With twain he coverèd his face,
And twain afore his feet did place,
And twain he had wherewith to fly,
And either did to other cry;
With 'Holy, Holy, Holy' both
Did bless the Lord of Sabaoth,
'His glory all the earth doth fill.'
Now at this voice, both loud and shrill,
The very door-posts shook apace,
And clouds of incense filled the place.

JESUS AND THE MOSS

(*In tiefster Schlucht im Waldesschooss.*)

Helmine *v.* Chezy, geb. *v.* Klenke.

Deep in the hollow of a wood
A moss-bed, green and spongy, stood,
   Like velvet-carpet soft:
To outward view, though scant and slight,
This nook contained a seemly sight
   Of leaves and boughs aloft.

To greenwood tree and rose o'erhead
The moss looked up and whisperèd,
   'Such bloom God gave me ne'er:
But trodden under foot of men
No worship my poor shrine doth ken,
   Mankind love light and glare.'

But lo! there came that even tide
Christ, roaming through the forest wide,
   With visage pale and wan:
Though footsore he would further go,
'Twas ease to feel the moss below
   His feet, the Son of Man.

Come o'er the plain in heat and thirst
In sand and sun, 'twas here that first
   The moss gan cool His feet.
Then spake the Lord, 'My Father's hand
'Such love in thee hath surely planned,
   'And made thee soft and sweet.

'What eye so blind as not to see
'E'en here in this thy low degree
   'God's power and grace and care?
'Thou comely herb, if set at nought,
'Of thee too thy Creator thought;
   'Thy lot serenely bear.'

Jesus had scarcely spoken so
When from the moss began to grow
   A rose, of wondrous hue:
Moss-rose 'twas called in little time,
It bloometh now in every clime,
   Of meekness emblem true.

SAINT JOHN AND THE LITTLE WORM

(*Johannes ging am hellen Bach*)
—Helmine *v.* Chezy.

JOHN, walking by a stream one day,
Beheld the crystal waters play;
Through greenwood, grass and flowers he trod:
He saw, and lift his heart to God.
How fresh the bloom, how fair the sight,
How beautiful the world and bright!
The blossoms, how they laugh and sing,
And verdant meadows tell of spring!
No herb on earth, no leaf on tree,
But trace their being, Lord, to thee:
Each little worm alive is fain,
And though the clothing ne'er so plain,
All, all that fan the vital spark
Of love divine bear stamp and mark.
The Saint was musing thus that tide,
When he a worm beneath him spied,
So gray and small that good Saint John
Had well-nigh set his foot thereon.
He picked her up from where she lay,
And perched her on a flowret gay,

'Thou ought'st to live, not die,' quoth he,
' The spring-field flowereth e'en for thee.'
The worm scarce felt his blissful touch,
But feeling it, her joy was such
That, fired with love and heart a-glow,
A lovely light she soon gan show,
And straight put forth of wings a pair,
Wherewith to journey through mid-air,
O'er tree-tops of a summer's night,
With lustre, like an emerald bright,
Her bed, the flowerets near and far,
All brightly deckt with many a star.
Thus she, in greenwood sweet and low,
In peace and love shall always glow.

BELSHAZZAR'S FEAST

Daniel v.

THE hour of midnight fast drew on:
In slumber deep lay Babylon,
All, save the palace of the King,
Whence came the sound of banqueting.
For yonder in the Kingly hall
Belshazzar kept high festival,
And there the King in rich array
And thousand lords and ladies gay
On couches sumptuous recline,
And quaff full cups of sparkling wine.
Meanwhile 'twas wonderful to hear
The music of the minstrel quire,
On dulcimer, harp, sackbut, lute,
Pipe, tabor, sawtry, horn, and flute:
The goblets clink, the palace doth ring
With shout and cheer, "Long live the King."
Then up and spake the self same tide,
All hot with wine, that prince of pride,
' Ho! lordings, listen every one;
' Behold the King of Babylon.'
Thus spake the fool, and gave behest
To fetch him out of royal chest
The sacred vessels, silver, gold,

(By Nabuchodonosor bold
Brought back with many a costly gem
From temple of Jerusalem),
That prince and wife and concubine
May drink with King Belshazzar wine.
Then drank they, at his sovran word,
Wine from the vessels of the Lord.
And king and people, mad with pride,
The Gods of silver glorified,
Of gold and brass and wood and stone
And iron, for their Gods alone—
But lo! before Belshazzar's eyes
That self-same hour in wonder-wise,
Upon the plaster of the wall,
Where stood the seven-branch can'stick tall,
There came forth, as I understand,
The fingers of an Angel-hand.
The heavenly scribe a legend wrote
Of awful, memorable note;
A change came o'er the Monarch's face,
Thoughts filled his guilty soul apace,
His joints and loins became unstrung,
Hair stood on end, head downward hung,
His knees smote one another fast:
Unmanned he stood and all aghast.
No Chaldee clerk (search all the land)
Could read the writing of that hand,
Till Daniel's prophetic soul,
Interpreting the mystic scroll,
Made *Mene*, *Tekel*, *Peres* plain:——
That night was proud Belshazzar slain.

DIE EILE DER ZEIT IN GOTT

Des Knaben Wunderhorn.

THE Commandant at Gross-wardine
An only daughter had, long syne:
Theresa was her Christen name,
Chaste, godly she, and void of blame.

This maid to piety in sooth
Was given from her very youth.
She prayed and sang both day and night,
The praise of God her sole delight.

With holy joy and love a-flame,
Her face lit up at Jesu's Name;
In all her matters He was Guide,
And she His leal betrothèd bride.

A noble lord soon came to woo;
Her father gave consent thereto:
Her mother said, 'Theresa, pray,
'To such a suitor say not nay!

'O mother mine,' the daughter spake,
'I cannot him to husband take;
Lo! One already I have found,
Am to a heavenly Bridegroom bound.'

The mother said, 'Ah! daughter mine,
Cross not my wish, and father thine:
Both he and I are now grown old,
And blest by God with goods and gold.'

The daughter then 'gan weep and moan,
'I have a Bridegoom, all mine own,
To whom I sware, with promise good,
To keep my crown of maidenhood.'

The father said, 'This cannot be,
Dear child, I can in no-wise see
What will become of thee, anon,
When we old folks be dead and gone.'

The noble lord is back agen,
They fix the wedding, where and when:
That day, when all was ready, lo!
The bride elect was full of woe.

Off to her garden early she,
And there fell down on bended knee,
With heart and soul aloud 'gan call
On Jesus, best of bridegrooms all.

Upon her face the damsel lay,
For Jesus yearning oft that day,
Then did her well-beloved appear,
And said, 'My bride, lo! I am here.

DIE EILE DER ZEIT IN GOTT

'In little time thou verily
Shalt be in Paradise with me,
And there with Angels bright and fair
My greater joy and pleasure share.'

He greeted her in wondrous wise,
With shame-fastness she fain would rise,
Then closing to her eyelids twain,
She welcomed Jesus Christ again.

Her Lord then spake in words untold,
And gave her there a ring, of gold:
'Herein, my bride, love's token see,
This on thy finger wear for me.'

Came back the maid with roses sweet,
'O heavenly Bridegroom, thee I greet:
Herewith I thee my worship show,
None other love my heart shall know.'

These lovers twain upon their way
Pick many a floweret bright and gay,
Then Jesus spake unto his bride,
'Come, walk now in my Garden wide.'

He took the Damsel by the hand,
And led her to his native land;
Within his Father's garden fair
Stood roses many, rich and rare.

The maiden then in joy did haste
Of divers dainty fruits to taste:
No human fancy yet can know
What goodly fruit doth yonder grow.

She heard sweet musick, chant and song,
The time and while seemed nothing long.
And silvern streamlets, far and near,
Ran, e'en as crystal, bright and clear.

Then spake the Bridegroom to the Bride,
'Now thou hast viewed my Garden wide:
'Tis time to earth again to wend,
An angel shall thy steps attend.'

Wo was the maid to say farewell;
They reach the place where she did dwell,
The watchmen ask, 'who might she be?'
'I seek my father's house,' quod she.

'Thy father's name, pray who is he?'
'The Commandant' her answer free:
One of the watchmen spake and smiled,
'The Commandant hath ne'er a child.'

Her clothing plainly told that she
Was, as by birth, of high degree:
A watchman led her therewithal
Off to the City council-hall.

The burgesses much marvellèd,
Whence came she, and where born and bred.
Her father's family and name?
Pray let her straight declare the same.

They search the archives of the place,
And find! 'mid other things, a case
Where bride was lost, in auld lang syne,
Within this town of Grosswardine.

They count the time, and it was lo!
Hundred and twenty years ago:
And yet the maid was young and sheen,
And just as though she were fifteen.

Whereby the Council understand
It is the work of God's own hand:
Before the damsel meat they place,
But snow-white, pallid grew her face.

'Nought for my body more, I need,
But fetch me hither a priest in speed.
That so, or ere the world I leave
The Sacrament I may receive.'

Now soon as ever this was done,
And Christens saw it, many one,
Without a pang of anguish deep,
The maiden gently fell on sleep.

WACHET AUF, RUFFT UNS DIE STIMME

P. Nikolai.

W<small>AKE</small>! awake! from highest steeple
The watchmen cry, 'Awake ye people,
  'O Salem, from thy slumber rise,'
Midnight sleepers much in wonder
Hear their voices loud as thunder,
  Where, where are ye, O virgins wise?
Up! lamps in hand await
The bridegroom at the gate.   Alleluya.
  Let every guest in wedding vest
  Go forth to meet him, and be blest.

Syon hears these timely voices,
And hearing in her heart rejoices;
  Awake and on her feet anon.
Came the Spouse from heaven's city,
In truth effulgent, strong to pity:
  Her star arose, her light out-shone.
To Earth, thou worthy Crown,
Christ, Son of God, come down.   Hosianna.
  Fain would we all to thy glad hall
  Ascend and sup with thee withal.

WACHET AUF

Praise to thee, O King of heaven,
By men and Angel-tongues be given;
  Let harp and cymbal loud resound.
Syon hath twelve pearly portals,
Wherein with Angel-quires we mortals
  On high may stand thy throne around:
No eye hath seen the sight,
As yet, of such delight, Nor ear heard tell.
  Sing high, sing low, *Iö, Iö*
  Alway *in dulci jubilo.*

GOOD CHRISTEN MEN, 'TIS TIME TO SING

After *Nun lasst uns singen, dann es ist Zeit Paderborn,* 1609.

Good Christen men, 'tis time to sing,
    Est puer natus hodie:
Tis the birth-day of our King,
    Jesus Christus nomine,
Hodie, hodie,
Natus est rex glorie.

At Bethlehem when God was born,
    De stella sol iusticie,
Angels sang that happy morn
    Cum Maria Virgine.
Plaudite, plaudite,
    Dies est leticie.

The Shepherds haste and leave their flocks,
    Nam Christus natus hodie,
Find Him, laid by ass and ox
    De Maria Virgine.
Rex, ave! Rex, ave!
Rex eterne glorie.

From Saba far come princes three,
    Jam lucis orto sydere,
Low to fall on bended knee,
    Coram novo principe :
Triplice, triplice
Veniunt cum munere.

Ah! wo is me, sweet Babe for thee,
    Qui natus es de Virgine ;
Thou wilt die upon the tree
    Pro reorum crimine.
Utique, utique
    Parce nobis, Domine.

Yon bright-red berries tell, I ween,
    Jesu, de tuo sanguine,
Holly too hath prickles keen,
    Veni, coronabere.
Jesule, Jesule,
    Homo tu miserie.

But dead and buried though thou be,
    Miserrimo pro homine,
Thou shalt rise in morrows three,
    Nostro pro solamine.
Itaque, itaque
Vos redempti, psallite,

Now bells be rung and mass be sung,
    Est puer natus hodie,

Men and maidens, old and young,
    Eya, benedicite :
Gaudete, gaudete
    Cum Maria Virgine.

With Angels, herds and kings sing we
    Gloria tibi, Domine,
Born to-day of Saint Marie,
    Pro peccante homine.
Itaque, itaque
    Exultemus hodie.

A CHRISTMAS TREE

German.

As fast asleep I lay one night,
    I saw in front of me
Upon our floor a wonder-sight,
    A giant Christmas-tree.

From branches, like to break in two,
    Great golden apples hung:
A blaze of tapers red and blue
    Burnt brightly all among.

Sweet sugar-candy dolls were there
    Bedeckt in rich array.
And toys that boys and maidens fair
    Go wild wherewith to play.

Now while in mute amaze I stood,
    And fondly gazed thereon,
One apple good to eat I would,
    But—tree and all was gone.

I woke up from my dream, Ah! me
    'Twas darkness all around:
Cried I, dear lovely Christmas-tree,
    Say where thou may'st be found.

Then, as was meet, came answer plain,
   'Child, innocency keep:
Soon I shall visit thee again,
   Meantime, go off to sleep.

If thou be buxom, meek and mild,
   Thy dream fulfill'd shall be:
Babe Jesus, He will give thee, child,
   The fairest Christmas-tree.'

IN CRUCIS PENDENS STIPITE

Da Christus an dem Kreuze stund.

While Jesus hung upon the rood,
From head to foot bestained with blood,
   In pain surpassing measure,
Seven words spake he of charity
   For Christendom to treasure.

At first he said with gentle cheer
' Forgive their trespass, Father dear,
   Nor hold it in memory;
Did they but know, they ne'er would do
   To death the King of glory.'

See next, the dying thief hard by,
Bewailing sore his villany,
   In mercy Christ hath shriven.
' Thou verilie shalt be with me
   In Paradise ere even.'

Now Mary stood the cross beside:
' O Lady, see thy Son,' he cried,
   ' In John, my friend and brother:
And thou, O John, from this day on
   Take Mary to thy mother.'

Forth from his parchèd lips there burst
A wonder-cry, he saith 'I thirst,'
   The Lord of all creation
In midst of his own agonies
   Doth thirst for our salvation.

In bitter pain the Son divine
Saith, 'Eli, Eli, Father mine,
   Why hast thou me forsaken?'
What time we die, good Lord, be nigh,
   At doomsday us awaken.

The ninth hour come ('twas dark as night,
So gospel saith, and saith aright)
   ''Tis over,' hear him crying:
In awful strife the Lord of life
   Defeated death by dying.

Once more he spake afore the end,
'My spirit now I do commend,
   O Father, to thy keeping':
He cried aloud, his forehead bowed,
   Then gently fell on sleeping.

O sinner, learn thy lust to quell;
With contrite heart consider well
   These words of Jesus seven:
If haply he who died for thee
   May grant thee bliss in heaven.

HOLY CHURCH MUST RAISE THE LAY

After *Carmen suo dilecto*.

HOLY Church must raise the lay
    Of triumphal gladness;
Bride of Christ must doff to-day
    Robe of Lenten sadness:
Hark! from belfry tower and steeple
    Merry bells are ringing:
Ye must likewise, priests and people,
    Break forth into singing.

Man shall leave (so saith the book)
    Father eke and mother;
Christ his Father left and took
    Flesh of man, our brother:
See, O Church, the Lord of heaven,
    (Synagogue forsaken)
Unto thee his troth hath given,
    Thee to wife hath taken.

From the Bridegroom's riven side
    Blood and water flowing,—
Sacraments pre-signified,
    Grace to man bestowing:

Wooden ark doth safely cherish
  Noë's sons and daughters,
While the disobedient perish
  In the deluge-waters.

Samson until midnight lay,
  Gaza's guards despising:
While men slept, he bore away
  Gates and bars, arising:
David to his brethren goeth,
  And, on God reliant,
With a sling and stone o'erthroweth
  Goliath the giant.

Adam in a garden fell:
  In a garden Jesus
(Second Adam he) from hell
  Meetly doth release us:
Therefore fear no more, ye mortals,
  Satan arch-deceiver;
Christ doth open Eden's portals
  To the true believer.

Mone, I. f. 216.

CHRISTUS PRO NOBIS PASSUS EST

Piae Cantiones, 1582.

For us did Christ endure the pain,
For us the Lamb of God was slain:
For us he shed on holy rood
Of Calvary his life-red Blood:
So tolling by his death the knell
Of Satan's empire strong and fell.

Now, rising from the dead to-day,
He sped like victor from the fray:
And blotted out the heavy score
That stood against mankind of yore:
See Satan stript, that Prince of pride,
And gate of heaven flung open wide.

Hence cometh it to pass that we
Win access to the Father free,
Through Jesus Christ his only Son,
For man who unto death was done.
With Alleluya evermo
Benedicamus Domino.

TO-DAY WE TELL THE STORY

Rex omnipotens die hodierna.

To-day we tell the story,
   How, conquer'd death and hell,
Jesus, the King of glory,
   Went up in heav'n to dwell:
   But, forty days full clear,
Of holy Church and heaven,
Spake he unto th' Eleven,
   And spake as ye shall hear.

' Receive,' said he, ' my blessing,
   The kiss of peace thereto:
Go forth, your Lord confessing
   The wide world thro' and thro':
   Go, sinners bind, or free;
Cleanse in baptismal waters
All Adam's sons and daughters
   In Name of Trinity.'

' At Salem here abiding,
   Not many days at most,
According to my tiding
   Wait ye the holy Ghost:

Him shall the Father send:
Then go, the Gospel preaching,
First Jew, then Gentile teaching
To earth's remotest end.'

But lo! a cloud 'gan sunder
  Christ from th' Apostles' eyes:
Him they behold in wonder
  Ascending to the skies:
  These men of Galilee,
As upward they stand gazing
Upon the sight amazing,
  Two white-robed Angels see.

' Good sirs, why stand ye straining
  Into the clear blue sky?
He sits in glory reigning
  At God's right hand on high:
  This self-same Jesus so
Shall come in clouds of glory,
(It is no idle story)
  As ye have seen him go.'

Sovereign of all thy creatures,
  Whom sky, sea, earth, obey,
Thou after thine own features
  Mankind didst form of clay:
  Soon Satan full of guile,
Led captive us poor mortals,
And shut for men the portals
  Of Paradise awhile.

But see, thy crimson raiment
   Doth plainly testify
That thou hast made full payment
   For man's iniquity :
   To Paradise again,
From whence we were ejected,
Uplift thy folk elected,
   Draw, draw us in thy train.

Christ, at thy next appearing,
   To deem the quick and dead,
May words to work our cheering
   To us by thee be said :
   Where seemly Angels sing,
Mid realms of light supernal,
May we in songs eternal
   Praise thee, of heaven King.

Sequence, probably by Herman Contract, xi. cent.

GOD IS GONE UP ON HIGH TO-DAY

Celos ascendit hodie.

GOD is gone up on high to-day, Alleluya,
Jesus the King of bliss for aye : All. All. All.

Set at the Father's own right hand, Alleluya,
Sov'reign of sky, and sea, and land.   All.   All.   All.

The words of David, all and some, Alleluya,
In very sooth, to pass are come.   All.   All.   All.

My Lord now with the Lord doth sit, Alleluya,
High on his heavenly throne, to wit.   All.   All.   All.

Now Christ hath vanquish'd every foe, Alleluya,
Benedicamus Domino.   Alleluya, Alleluya, Alleluya.

To holy Trinity give praise, Alleluya,
With *Deo gracias* always.   Alleluya, Alleluya, Alleluya.

HARVEST-SONG

Es ist ein Schnitter, der heisst Tod.—*Wunderhorn f.* 40.

THERE is a Reaper, Death by name,
If power he hath, from God it came.
Now whetteth he sickle
To mow small and mickle,
Our turn 'tis to-morrow,
No 'scape; more the sorrow:
    Floweret fair, take care, beware.

The grass, so green and fresh to-day,
Full low to-morrow Death will lay.
Anemone, lily,
Pink, daffodown-dilly,
Marsh-marigold, tansy,
Forget-me-not, pansy.
    Floweret fair, take care, beware.

Full many myriad blossoms blithe
Have fallen victims to his scythe.
Ye flowers of the garden,
Death doth his heart harden.
Though never so pretty,
Here look not for pity.
    Floweret fair, take care, beware.

Tulips of white or yellow hue,
Ye silvern bells and borage blue,
Gay poppy and mallow,
Night-primula sallow,
Gorse, bonnie broom, heather,
Soon fade ye and wither.
    Floweret fair, take care, beware.

Fritillary and rose-marie,
Musk, honey-suckle, ambrosie,
Narcissus, germander,
Sweet-pea, oleander,
Of you and fresh roses
He soon will make posies;
    Floweret fair, take care, beware.

Yet, welcome, Death, I fear thee nought,
Thrust in thy sickle, quick as thought.
Thou slayest me, granted;
'Tis but to be planted
In heavenly bowers,
The country of flowers,
    Floweret fair, be glad, not sad.

SPINN, MÄDCHEN, SPINN

Spin, Maiden, spin,
And thus more wisdom win:
As thy golden tresses lengthen,
So shall age thy prudence strengthen.

Praise, Maiden, praise
The loom of olden days:
Adam delved and Eva span;—
Pattern to the sons of man.

Hie! Maiden, hie!
Like Anna, distaff ply:
She by spinning skilled to find
Sustenance for Tobit blind.

Laud, Maiden, laud:
Our Lady's ways applaud.
Oft she wove, that Mother mild,
Garments for the Holy Child.

Sing, Maiden, sing;
To virtue closely cling:
All thy mind to spinning lend,
Good beginning make good end.

SPINN, MÄDCHEN, SPINN

Learn, Maiden, learn
Thy happiness eterne:
Learn, while thou thy wheel dost tread,
Word of God, and holy dread.

Trust, Maiden, trust:
Thy life, it is but dust.
Quickly thou must join the dead,
Broken be thy silver thread.

Joy! Maiden, joy!
Thy gold be *sans* alloy!
So thy Faith and Hope shall wax
Like thy yarn, and like thy flax.

Bless, Maiden, bless
Thy God for healthfulness,
Strength to turn, in woe or weal,
This thy busy spinning-wheel.

SUMMER

Geh 'aus mein Herz und suche Freud—Leipzig
Gesangbuch, nr. 495.

Go out, my heart, and seek delight:
Of God's good gifts go view the sight
   This lovely summer-morning.
'Twill make our spirits blithe and glad
To see the gardens freshly clad
   In nature's rich adorning.

The greenwood tree hath leafage new,
The fields are deckt in verdant hue,
   May-blossoms thickly cluster:
Not Solomon in rich array
With lily white or tulip gay
   Could vie, for grace and lustre.

The lark doth sing and soar aloft,
From rocky cleft the turtle oft
   To wood-ward forth doth sally:
That songster-king, the nightingale
With warbling throat doth fill the dale,
   And holt and heath and valley.

Hen marcheth forth with chicken small:
The stork hath nested on the wall;
　　Doth feed her young the swallow.
Now leave the hills for meadows low,
And pastures green, the bounding roe,
　　The dun deer and the fallow.

Swift streamlets prattle o'er the strand,
And paint the banks on either hand
　　With myrtle-shadows pleasant:
The meads hard-by resound agen
With songs of merry shepherd-men,
　　And bleating sheep incessant.

The busy bees they come and go
In countless number to and fro
　　In quest of honey-treasure:
Sweet vine-sap in the month of May
Fresh virtue gaineth day by day,
　　In slow but certain measure.

The growing crops upon the land
Make young and old to clap the hand,
　　The goodness great confessing
Of Him who feedeth flock and pen,
And showereth on the sons of men
　　Full many a priceless blessing.

Myself, I cannot silence keep,
God's works so manifold and deep

SUMMER

My soul doth inly ponder
In chorus with the rest I sing
And while o'er earth his praises ring,
   I praise him too in wonder.

Methinks, if here thou art so fair,
So kind to man and debonair
   In these poor earthly bowers,
What then hereafter wilt thou be
In heaven itself, that rich citie
   Of golden streets and towers.

What pleasure high, what sunshine bright,
In Christ's own garden, day and night,
   To hear the bells a-ringing:
Where all unite to swell the hymn
Of Cherubim and Seraphim
   Sweet Alleluyas singing.

Would God that I were there to stand
With palm-branch in my either hand,
   Before thy presence bending:
So then would I in Angel-wise
Extol thy Name above the skies
   In Antiphons unending.

Meantime, good Lord, till hence I fare,
While soul her body's yoke must bear,
   Be thou my theme and story:
Yea, more and more my heart from now
In this and every place shall bow
   In awe before thy glory.

Did but my drooping spirit know
The blessings that from heaven do flow,
   My flowers were fresh and pearly:
Make thou my soul thy garden-field,
Ripe summer-fruits of grace to yield
   With faith both late and early.

Make room for thine own Spirit free,
So shall I wax a goodly tree,
   And strike my roots the lower:
O help me for thy greater praise
To bide throughout my length of days
   Thy lovesome plant and flower.

Be Paradise, nay, Heaven my goal:
Transplant me thither body, soul,
   Bedeckt in vesture vernal.
To thee my God and other none
My homage now and aye be done
   In songs of praise eternal.

Paul Gerhardt.

A PRAYER TO BE SAID ON GOING TO BED

O Ihësu dulcissime.

O JESU, honey to my heart,
My well-belovèd thou that art,
Nay, prithee, tarry by my side,
The livelong night with me abide.
And though mine eyelids slumber take,
My heart to thee be aye awake:
And while she keepeth vigil still,
Thy presence, Lord, my soul fulfil,
My shield from every kind of ill.

My body-guard thine Angels be,
Thy cross for safety stamped on me.
Let Satan flee far, far away,
And Jesus only with me stay.
My kith and kindred, mighty King,
Guard under covert of thy wing:
Ah! leave not them, nor me forsake,
But ever in thy keeping take,
And bless us sleeping or awake.

A Hymner at Freiburg, no. 91 *f.* 48 *xv. cent.*

III

THE LEGEND OF SAINT DOROTHY

THE LEGEND OF SAINT DOROTHY, VIRGIN AND MARTYR

THREE hundred winters, less or more,
Had come and gone since Gabriel bore
Our Lady tiding of the birth
Of Jesus, King of heaven and earth,
When early in one year befel
The things whereof I now will tell.

In Cappadocia's chiefest town,
Hight Cæsarea, of renown,
There dwelt a maiden, fair of face,
Young, virtuous and full of grace.
Of noble strain and high degree
Descended was this maiden free,
Her father's name, I know it not,
Nor yet her mother's, God them wot.
But righteous folk were they, I trow,
And Christen, though 'twas not as now
An easy and a common thing
To own the Faith of Christ the King;
Nor had that hill-countree and coast
Heard tell of God the Holy Ghost,
Yet when this maiden child was born,
Unheeding foes and heathen scorn,

These parents good, with God-sips three,
In Name of Holy Trinity,
As taught by Mother Church, in water
Did christen this their little daughter.
Full well knew they, that children young,
As David in his Psalter sung,
Are heritage and gift of love
From God omnipotent above,
So when they to the font-stone came,
They gave her Dorothy to name,
For *Doron*, if I wish to speak,
Is *Gift*, and *Theos God*, in Greek.

Soon, early piety to foster,
The maid was taught her *Paternoster*
And learnt by heart the Apostles' Creed
With *Ave Marie*, and loved to read
The word of holy writ and sing
The praise of Christ, the Infant King.
While still a child, 'twas her delight
To fast, and pray morn, noon and night.
Nor could she too much honour pay
To Jesus Christ's arising day,
And every first day of the week
His altar she would early seek,
There to receive, with good intent,
The venerable Sacrament.
So strengthened by this food divine,
The consecrated Bread and Wine,
Fair Dorothy year after year
Did grow in grace and holy fear,

In favour both with God and man.
At home she daily sat and span
Thick woollen garments for the old
For greater warmth in weather cold.
Well wot she, as Saint Jacob taught,
Faith void of works is good for naught.
And well aware that idleness
Is nurse of vices, more or less,
Therefore this blissful Dorothy
Was ever busy as a bee,
A-working with her hands for other,
Some sister sick, or needy brother.
So when she passed along the street,
In winter or in summer heat,
The widow and the agèd poor
At window or at open door
Would rise and call the damsel blest,
Her fame was known by east and west,
For 'twas her meat and drink to cherish
Whoso were like to starve and perish.

About that time, the Fiend of hell,
As history of Church doth tell,
Stirred up at Rome, a heathen man,
The tyrant Diocletïan,
To persecute with fire and sword
The worshippers of Christ the Lord.
Throughout the empire quickly spread
The tidings of this order dread.
No persecution till then
Was half so fierce, for maids and men,

Babe, elder, husband, wife and daughter
Were haled to prison and to slaughter:
For 'twas the Emperor's decree,
And eke the will of Paganie,
Wherever Christen might be found,
Alike above or under ground,
Either to force them, every one,
To worship Gods of wood and stone;
Or failing this, the penalty
Was first to suffer, then to die.
Thus did the heathen vent their spleen
On such as owned the Nazarene:
So, *Christianos ad leones,*
Et Christianas ad lenones.

In course a time there came a brief
To Cæsarea's head and chief,
Fabricius, and lief or lothe,
This Governor was bound by oath
To do his Emperor's behest.
And this he did anon with zest;
For he too was a pagan bold
Nor did with Christen people hold,
And straightway he did summon all
Poor Christen to his judge-ment hall,
As many as were in that city,
I ween, he showed them little pity.
Along with whom, as I you say,
Came Dorothy, that lovely may.
Fabricius had long heard tell
Concerning yonder damosel,

And now he saw her face to face,
No fairer maid in all that place.
There stood she, Dorothy the sheen,
Of noble form and modest mien
Adornèd not with plaited hair,
Nor decked with jewels rich and rare,
Nor dight with ornaments of gold,
Like many a heathen damsel bold.
She was not clad in rich array,
In silken robe or satin gay,
But rather, like the Saints of yore,
Apparel neat and plain she wore,
Full well she knew that clothes withal
Are badge and token of the Fall,
'And love of dress did ne'er begin
Till Eve our mother learnt to sin,'
And being ware that garments came
At first, in part to cover shame,
And partly to protect from cold
Our bodies, be we young or old,
So Dorothy was well content
With simple, neat habiliment,
And satisfied, if she might be
Clad inly with humility,
And with that meek and quiet spirit
That doth the praise of heaven merit.

In robes of virtue thus arrayed
Came Dorothy, and nought dismayed
Afore the Governour she stood,
Mirrour of saintly maidenhood.

Then spake Fabricius anon
As touching her religïon;
And Dorothy made plain reply,
'A Christen maiden, Sir, am I,
That worship Christ who died for me
Upon the Cross at Calvary.
And I will serve in life and death
This Jesus Christ of Nazareth.'
She spake, and straight Fabricius
In angry wise made answer thus.
'O silly maid, if thou dost mean,
Thou worshippest the Nazarene
The Emperor is no believer
Nor I myself in that deceiver.
And by our law and firm decree
Thou must renounce thy Christentie,
And prove the same by outward sign,
By burning incense at the shrine
Of great Diana, whom we here
With all in Asia revere.
Between two roads, then, take thy choice,
But, as I rede thee, hear my voice.
Curse him of Nazareth and so
Long life and pleasure thou shalt know.
But shouldèst thou prove stubborn still,
And disobey thy monarch's will,
A death of shameful agony,
Be sure, fond damsel, thou shalt die.'

'So be it!' quoth that maiden bright,
'The sooner then to see the sight,

And stand before the presence blest,
Of Him, whom I do love the best,
For whose dear sake, I dare well say,
I would lay down my life to-day.'

Then cried the Governour, ' How now ?
Explain thy word, whom meanest thou ? '
With gentle voice the maid replied,
' Sir, understand I am a bride,
Betrothèd to the Son of God,
Who years ago this planet trod ;
At Christmas in a stable born,
He lived in poverty and scorn ;
When thirty years and three were gone,
They crucified that Holy one :
He died and then was laid in grave,
His people upon earth to save,
But on the third day he full fain
From hell and death arose again,
And after forty days were ended,
Lo ! into heaven Christ ascended :
There with the Lord my Lord doth sit,
At God's the Father's side, to wit.
And thence upon the latter day
He shall descend (the sooth I say)
With wound-prints five, still fresh and red,
To bless or punish quick and dead.
Meanwhile my Lord, he doth prepare
A blissful home both bright and fair
In heavenly places, earth above,
For such as do the Master love.

Methinks that it were full great pity
To forfeit such a blessed city—
It hath to name Hierusalem—
Whose walls are built of many a gem,
Whose streets are paved with beaten gold,
And diamonds, of price untold,
With turrets tall of ivory,
And gates of pearl full fair to see,
There nought unclean may enter in,
Nor lie, nor any kind of sin;
No tear, no sigh, no sob, no groan;
Pain, sickness, death are there unknown.
They have no need of candle light,
'Tis alway day and never night.
My Master hath a garden there
Wherewith none other can compare.
No thorn or thistle there is seen,
But grass and trees are ever green.
There snowdrops blossom all year round,
Blue squills and marigolds abound,
While yellow crocus and sweet pea
Do blossom everlastingly.
There lilies white and roses red
Adorn full many a flowery bed.
There nightingales do alway sing,
For why, 'tis everlasting spring,
And birds of Paradise make merry
On spray of holly-tree or cherry—
And see within his orchard wall
Where grow the fruit-trees, choice and tall,

He, Jesus Christ, my Lover true,
Hath pomegranates of rosy hue.
Oft in his garden he will walk,
And with his well-belovèd talk:
He many a time and oft will pick
Fruit from a bough, with apples thick,
And bid us take and taste and see
How rich in grace our Lord can be:
Or else doth cull, to our delight,
Some ruby rose or lily white,
Wherewith to weave a wreathlet gay,
That ne'er can wither nor decay.
Ah! me, 'twere joy untold to bide
So near his heart and wounded side,
To dwell for aye in such a place,
And see my Saviour face to face.'

Thus nobly Dorothy and well:
Her judge's thoughts I cannot tell
For certain, but 'tis somewhere said
That he, enamoured of the maid,
To make her concubine or wife,
Would willingly have spared her life,
Struck by her eloquence and beauty,
Yet judge must needs perform his duty.
So willy, nilly, he at last
Death-sentence on the damsel passed,
Then bade his squires and knights so keen
Bind Dorothy the Nazarene,
And lodge her in a darksome cell
That lay below the citadel,

And there he hoped in little while,
By might or flattery or guile,
Either to gratify his lust,
Or make the Christen lick the dust,
Compelling her at any price
To do Diana sacrifice.

Alas! 'twere pitiful to tell
The malice of the powers of hell,
How Satan and his fiends assayed
To terrify or coax this maid.
But no appeal nor promise fair
Made by the enemy to spare
Her youthful life, no punishment
Could shake this Virgin's firm intent :
With more than courage of a man
The fight she fought, her course she ran.
In vain the scourge, the rack, the wheel,
For Dorothy was true as steel
To Jesus Christ, in weal and woe,
Undaunted or by friend or foe.
At length the fatal day was come
When she must suffer martyrdom :
Yet ne'er was bird of morning-light
More glad than she, that maiden bright :
But ere she started on her way,
Her orisons she first would say,
That Christ, a maiden's Son, might lend
A maiden patience to the end.
Eftsoon, of every sin forgiven,
And by her agèd Bishop shriven,

And houseled, and for aught I know,
Anealed with holy oil also,
She knelt adown to praise the Lord;
Though slain in body by the sword,
The foeman could not kill her soul;
That, *Deo gracias!* was whole.
And though she might in prison be,
To God her spirit still was free.
See now along the master-street
They lead that lamb : with willing feet
She fareth, on that morning chill,
To bleed upon the heading-hill.
The town crièr, O truth sublime!
Could charge her with no grievous crime.
For she had nothing done amiss,
Her utmost guilt lay but in this,
That, heedless she of death or danger,
Adored one cradled in a manger.
Thought many a heathen in that crowd,
Although not one durst speak aloud,
Whenas they heard the victim's name,
'Twere thousand pities, nay foul shame
To lift a hand or raise the tongue
Against a noble girl so young,
Though she were Christen, maid or wife,
Whose grace and alms and blameless life
Had won the love, as I have told,
Of rich and poor, sick, young and old.
But there were other in the throng,
Indifferent of right or wrong,

Idolaters, full well content
That maids should suffer punishment,
However good of life or bad,
Who being 'side themselves and mad,
For neither reason, rhyme nor cause
Defied both Cæsar and his laws:
So let them take the consequence
Of wilful disobedience.
And there were Pagans, not a few,
Alas! and here and there a Jew,
Come out of curiosity
To see a Christen woman die.
And some there were in game and glee
Made mock of hapless Dorothy,
And many a lewd and heartless man,
With gay and giddy courtezan,
In linen fine and purple drest,
Made unbecoming joke and jest.
God shrive them ere the judgement day,
Certain, they know not what they say.
Now, while they stopt awhile for breath,
The maiden and those men of death,
A youth, was had in great renown
In that citee, did chance adown
The hill to pass, on pleasure bent,
Or else on business intent,
For proto-notary was he,
A pagan, of his money free,
And ever open house he kept,
Theophilus he was y-clept.

Now, as it happened for to fall,
This wight was in the judgement hall
When Dorothy, upon her trial,
Said, sooner than make base denial
Of Jesus, she would suffer pain,
Nay death, if heaven she might but gain,
And walk in Paradise, that garden
Whereof her Bridegroom was the warden.
So when Theophilus drew nigh
And saw that maid led forth to die,
He lift his voice above the crowd
And cried in scorn, and laughter loud,
' Ha! Dorothy, fair maid, and so
To join thy Bridegroom thou dost go,
And dwell with him in Paradis.
Pray, send me from that place of bliss
A rosebud, either white or red,
Or apple newly gathered,
Or other fruit and flower in token
That thou the very sooth hast spoken,
For I would smell those roses sweet
And of his apples taste and eat.'
Then Dorothy uplift her eyes
And looked on him in loving wise,
And blest the scoffer, saying thus,
' Thy suit is heard, Theophilus : '
And thereupon both he and all
His merry comrades, great or small,
Did only laugh the louder still,
As on they journeyed down the hill.

She entering on the latest stage
Of that her earthly pilgrimage
And yearning for the happy home,
Abode of Hallows, all and some,
Again gan climb the dreadful steep,
To die, or rather fall a-sleep.
Yet when she saw the head-man stand
Beside the block, with axe in hand,
And viewed the crowd, the rabblement,
And every eye upon her bent,
Throughout her frame, so pale and wan,
A shiver for the moment ran,
But to her comfort lo! she spied
A heavenly boy stood by her side
Whose countenance was all a-glow,
With raiment white as driven snow,
Whose hair fell like a sunbeam bright,
His eyes did flash like thunder-light.
A basket in his hand had he,
Of flowerets, sweet and fair to see,
And he had brought a gift of fruit,
From princely stem and noble root;
Three roses newly gatherèd
From some delightsome garden-bed,
And apples three full ripe there were,
Fresh produce of some orchard rare.

Then Dorothy, the saintly maid,
At first became full sore afraid,
But when that she did understand
That he was sent from Angel-Land

To be a Comforter indeed,
And blessing in her hour of need,
'Hail! Seraph bright and fair,' she spake,
'Nay, prithee, now, for Jesus' sake,
Go, seek and find Theophilus,
And make him straightway one of us.
Go take these fruits and lovely flowers
And say they come from heavenly bowers,
Say, ' thitherward, the donor free,
The Christen maiden Dorothy,
Beyond the sun and stars and moon,
Doth journey very, very soon.'
And add ' (Please God) within a trice
She will be safe in Paradise,'
And lastly, 'she will 'wait him there.'
Then while that Angel debonaire
Did on his loving errand go
To seek Theophilus below,
Knelt Dorothy upon the sod
And lift both heart and voice to God
Praying for friends, and foes at large,
'This sin, Lord, lay not to their charge.'
Then bade her orisons full fast,
' Jesu, receive my soul at last.'
The blow is fallen—Lift your voice,
Ye heathen folk, rejoice, rejoice,
But know, the Martyr's blood indeed
Is Holy Church's fruitful seed,
Where much the husbandman hath sown,
The richest harvest there is mown.

And in the footsteps of yon Martyr
Shall many follow, glad to barter
Brief life on earth for endless rest
In Paradise amid the blest,
Led by her prayer and pattern bright
From shades of darkness into light.
This death an hundred-fold shall yield,
And first-fruit of this harvest-field
Theophilus anon shall be.
For scarcely had that maiden free,
And Martyr, drawn her latest breath,
And barely closed her eyes in death
When th' Angel Child, of whom I spake
Into the town his way did take
The Notary's abode to find,
And fleet he sped as western wind.
He found him, with his men of nought,
Still laughing at the very thought
Of Dorothea's promised gift.
Before him set the Angel swift
The basket full of fruit and flowers
So lately pickt from heavenly bowers,
And said, 'Fair fall you! an ye please,
See, Dorothy hath sent you these.'
And other words he spake thereto
E'en as the maiden bade him do,
Then vanished through the closèd door.
Theophilus, in wonder sore,
Then spake unto his fellows all
Assembled in his dining hall,

As writers of this legend tell,
And cried ' Farewell, a long farewell ;
That Christen maiden (blest be she!)
Hath kept her word in verity,
Henceforth the God, whoso be he,
Of Dorothy, my God shall be,
The which hath sent his Angel hither
From Paradise, to draw me thither.
Sooth, none but Jesus, Son of Mary,
Can ripen fruit in February,
And to his garden I must go,
Where all year round red roses blow.'
When he did scent those flowrets fair,
And tasted of the apples rare,
His heart became like melting wax,
No more of manners loose and lax :
He rewed what he had done amiss,
And suddenly new life was his.
And he that hitherto did scorn
The Name of Christ, again is born
Of water and the Holy Ghost,
At Easter-tide or Pentecost.
He after Dorothy's example,
Sin under foot did learn to trample ;
He too for Christ his life laid down,
Thus meriting a Martyr's crown.
And so-gate, as foretold it was
By Dorothy, it came to pass,
Now he with palm - branch in his
  hand
Beside this Martyr-maid doth stand.

May we too join her company,
And make good ending when we die :
Be ours to win that happy home,
The fields of Paradise to roam,
Where noble fruits and flowers abound,
And true and endless joys are found,
Where seemly Angels sit and sing
And merrily the bells do ring,
Where day and night the heavenly host
Bless Father, Son and Holy Ghost.   AMEN.

www.ingramcontent.com/pod-product-compliance
Lightning Source LLC
Chambersburg PA
CBHW030906170426
43193CB00009BA/753